Golf and the GOSPEL

Golf and the GOSPEL

HOW TO IMPROVE YOUR SCORE
in the GAME OF LIFE

R. BLAINE DETRICK

C.S.S. Publishing Company, Inc.
Lima, Ohio

GOLF AND THE GOSPEL

Library of Congress Cataloging in Publication Data

Detrick, R. Blaine, 1918-
Golf and the Gospel.

1. Christian life — Methodist authors. 2. Golf — Religious aspects — Christianity. I. Title.
BV4501.2.D493 1985 248.4 85-15184

5873 / ISBN 0-89536-766-1

PRINTED IN U.S.A.

Table of Contents

Foreword

The "Peanuts" comic strip is a favorite of mine — and of many of you. Some time ago, there was a strip where Linus, speaking to Charlie Brown, remarks, "My dad is a kind of philosopher. He says that the game of golf and the game of life are very similar."

Charlie Brown replies, "That is true."

Then, in the last panel, he adds, "Unfortunately, in the game of life, I'm always hitting from the back tees!"

Many of us can readily identify with Charlie Brown. We often feel exactly as he does.

Golf and life do parallel each other in many respects. At times the correlation is almost amazing. And these brief chapters will seek to explore the relationship between the two.

You will not need to understand anything about golf in order to appreciate this book. We'll be talking more about life than the links and more about God than about golf.

So if you are a golfer and expect to receive some good tips for improving your game, disillusion yourself. Go to a pro for this.

Let us hope, however, that your spiritual game will be improved. And let us also hope that some of the lessons from the golf course may be applied — yes, will be applied — in our hearts and in our lives.

1

“ Off The Tee”

Chapter One

As we begin, we start where any golfer does — off the tee. Whether he is a pro or a duffer, a golfer goes to the first tee and prepares to hit the ball. The drive from the tee is the opening stroke on every golf hole.

That first swing, that drive, is very important each time. Every golfer dreams of standing at the tee after he has driven and watching the ball sail long and high and straight, right down the middle of the fairway, 200 yards or more! That's a great start! What a lift to begin with a good drive.

Unfortunately, it does not always happen that way. I speak from experience. Instead of the ball going straight, quite often it is pulled to the left or sliced to the right. Or worse yet, sometimes I top the ball and it just dribbles out a bit, only about twenty or thirty yards. This can be embarrassing and humiliating.

Some time ago, while playing with a man who is an excellent golfer, who really hits the ball well, I was having one of those bad days. On each of the first three holes, when driving off the tee, I just rolled the ball a few yards out in front of the tee.

After the third time, he turned to me and said in a helpful sort of way, “I think I know what part of your trouble is. You're standing too close to the ball — after you hit it!”

The drive off the tee gives the golfer either a good or a bad start. To a large extent, it dictates the way in which the rest of the hole will be played. That drive, that beginning, is very important. This is the emphasis I want to make right now.

First let me apparently reverse myself and add this: even though the beginning is important, it isn't everything. You still must continue to play; you still have to finish the hole. And it is possible to have a good drive and waste it. Likewise, it is possible to have a poor drive and overcome it.

Let me speak from personal experience again. Those of you who are golfers can appreciate this. I have had those times when the drive went straight down the middle, when it was long and far, straight and true. I would walk out to the ball for the second shot and think to myself, “Boy, I've got this hole under control now.” Overconfidence. And then I would dub the next shot, or hit into the trees, or put the ball in a sand trap, or skid it over the green, or three-putt the green. Many a time have I had a good drive and ended up with a poor score: a double bogey, or worse; a seven or an eight, or more. So a fine drive can be wasted.

On the other hand, it is possible to have a poor drive and overcome it. I still remember one particular time, when I had a worthless drive, one of those that just rolled a short distance. And it was a par five hole. But I hit a beautiful second shot, then put the third shot on the green. And then dropped the putt! That's four strokes on a par five — so I had a birdie, one under par! I remember that hole well! I never forget a hole like that. This happens so rarely that it leaves a lasting impression and is tucked away in my memory permanently.

So it is possible to have a good drive and waste it. And it is possible to have a poor drive and still recover from it.

As it is in golf, so it is in life. And so it is in your spiritual experience. A good beginning is very important. But — it is possible to have a good beginning and waste it; it is possible to have a poor beginning and overcome it.

Here then are two phrases to remember right now: 1) A good beginning can be ruined, and 2) A poor beginning can be redeemed.

Let's take an illustration of each of these from the pages of the Bible, one from the Old Testament, one from the New Testament.

A Good Beginning Can Be Ruined – Saul, Son of Kish

In the Old Testament there is a story about a man named Saul — Saul, the son of Kish; Saul, the first king of Israel.

Our first impression of this man is very favorable. In our initial encounter with Saul, the son of Kish, he was hunting for his father's lost donkeys (1 Samuel 9:1-3). The donkeys had wandered away, so Saul took a servant and together they went out to try to find the donkeys. What an impression young Saul made. He was a tall man; the Bible says that he stood head and shoulders above anyone else in his tribe (9:2; 10:23).

He was handsome, hard-working, diligent. He hunted for those donkeys so long that his dad thought he was lost and was extremely anxious about him (10:2). Saul wanted to finish what he started to do. He was thorough and persevering.

He was also humble. While he was being selected as the first king of Israel, he was not in the public eye, like most politicians: campaigning for himself, shaking hands, slapping backs, kissing babies, making promises. He was hiding amid the supplies and equipment, the baggage of the camp (10:22). After the people chose him to be king, they had to go hunt for him — and almost drag him out into the open. He was humble, shy, retiring.

"What do you mean, 'Samuel anointed you to be king instead of me'?"

Saul was also a courageous man. He had not been king very long before an emergency arose. One of the cities (Jabesh-Gilead) on the border toward Ammon was being beseiged and asked for help. Saul gathered together his armies, recruiting men from all of the tribes. A battle was fought and a victory was won, against great odds (11:1-11). He was a fearless, bold leader.

Saul was diligent; he was humble; he was courageous. He was also very compassionate. Even though the Lord himself had put his finger upon this man to be the first king, not everybody was in favor of his selection (10:27). Nobody achieves a top position without some opposition and competition. And in those days, when you got to the top, you eliminated your competition. When you became king, or ruler, those who had stood in your way were to be killed. This seems harsh and cruel to us, but it was a way of life back then. Everybody took it for granted.

We don't do things quite the same way today. If the Democrats win an election, they do not kill all the Republicans. Nor do the Republicans, if they win, kill all the Democrats. We are a little more civilized today — we secure our position and maintain our control in various other ways. Of course, in some parts of the world, there are people — and nations — who still live by this Old Testamant practice.

But after Saul became king, he said, "No, no — let my opponents live. There will be no more slaughter today" (11:12, 13). This was on the day of his first great victory.

So here is a man who leaves a tremendous first impression; he is off to an outstanding start. You cannot help but admire him: his imposing appearance, his diligence, his humility, his courage, his compassion. He is an ideal choice to be the first king of Israel.

His career reached a peak and then started downhill. It is a degrading story to read some of the experiences of King Saul. Success and achievement went to his head. Why does this happen so often? He became overly ambitious and arrogant. Envy and greed, suspicion and jealousy began to take hold of him. He did things that earlier in his life he would never have done. His life filled with despair. No one could have been off to a better start — yet he made a fool of himself.

The passage from the Scriptures telling of his selection as king was from the tenth chapter of 1 Samuel. Now let us move ahead to chapter thirteen. We discover Saul was anxious to get into battle, this time against the Philistines. Saul and his men were ready. But Samuel, the priest, had said, "Wait at Gilgal seven days, and I will be there to offer the sacrifice." Saul waited and waited. The Philistines became more threatening. And Saul grew more nervous and impatient. Finally, on the seventh day, Samuel still had not come. So Saul took it upon himself to make the sacrificial offering. This was an act which only the priest of the holy God could do. But Saul decided to do it. Almost immediately, Samuel arrived. Saul was severely rebuked (13:8-14). His deterioration had begun.

Now we move forward to chapter fourteen. And we find the story of the victory against the Philistines.

Before the battle, Saul had done another foolish thing. He had ordered his army to fast; no one was to eat any food, all day long (14:24). In the morning, the army defeated the Philistines and had them on the run. They could not, however, follow through on their triumph because they became weak, for lack of nourishment (14:28-31). A golden opportunity for a crushing victory was lost — because they couldn't follow through, because of Saul's stupid and ridiculous order.

However, Jonathan, his son, had left camp earlier in the morning with his armor-bearer, before Saul's command was issued. They slipped behind the Philistine lines, and won an unexpected conflict (14:1-14). Along with a timely earthquake (14:15), Jonathan was really responsible for the panic and confusion which provided the opportunity for the Israelites' stunning defeat of the enemy.

On the way back to camp, Jonathan saw some wild honey. He was hungry. He scooped up some of it and ate it. He did not know of his father's orders (14:27).

But when Saul learned what had happened, he said, "Jonathan must die." His own son, the man responsible for the surprise victory that day. For disobeying orders he had never heard.

The people rose up in indignation against King Saul. They refused to permit the slaying of Jonathan. They would not allow Saul to do it (14:43-45). Jonathan was spared, but we see the continuing decline of one who had been off to a great start.

Now we continue to 1 Samuel 15 (this is the third consecutive chapter where Saul's decay is pictured). The Lord, through Samuel, had given Saul definite and specific orders in a particular situation. But Saul turned right around and did exactly the opposite. He flagrantly, intentionally, and deliberately disobeyed God. After this, Samuel came to him in the name of the Lord and said, "Your kingdom will be taken from you" (15:1-23). Saul's deterioration was complete.

Thus the career of this man, who had such a wonderful beginning, reached its climax, then disintegrated and decayed until it collapsed in despair, defeat, and death. The Philistines finally conquered him, and in a final battle at Gilboa (chapter thirty-one), both Saul and Jonathan died. Saul finished about as low as can be imagined — a disgraceful suicide. A fine start — but a foolish and futile end. A good beginning can be ruined.

A Poor Beginning Can Be Redeemed — Saul, Of Tarsus

Let us now turn over to the pages of the New Testament. We find another man with the same name, Saul. Saul, of Tarsus.

What is our first impression of him? The first time in the Bible that we met Saul of Tarsus, he was one of the bad guys, from a Christian point of view.

In our initial look at Saul, he was consenting to the death of Stephen, the first Christian martyr. He was watching the coats of the witnesses (Acts 7:58), encouraging the people to throw their rocks at Stephen and stone him to death. Saul of Tarsus then became the leader of the opposition movement. Saul led the group that broke into the homes of those who were suspected of being Christians. He dragged them out, arrested them, whipped them, imprisoned them, hounded them, drove them from the city, murdered them — even women and children. His one goal was simply to wipe Christianity from the face of the earth, to exterminate and destroy these people who followed Jesus. He was the supreme persecutor, the unsurpassed enemy of the early church. What a most distasteful and repugnant beginning — torturing, flogging, and slaughtering Christian believers (8:3, 9:1).

Then one day he took a journey to the city of Damascus, and we all know what happened. He was on his way to Damascus because there were not enough Christians left in Jerusalem for him to persecute; he had driven away practically all of them.

So he headed north toward Damascus to do the same thing there — persecute, imprison, and torture the followers of Jesus.

Just outside the city, right in the middle of the day, a bright light shone out of the heavens. He was blinded and driven to his knees. In his darkness, he heard the voice of the Lord (9:1-9).

From that experience, Saul of Tarsus was literally transformed. The whole direction of his life was changed. He became the man we know as Paul, the apostle. From Saul of Tarsus to Paul the apostle. He became the man who wrote half the books in our New Testamant. He became the man who is probably the greatest missionary the Christian Church has ever known. He became the man who is noted as an outstanding Christian, a preeminent leader of the faith, an unequalled spokesman for the Lord Jesus Christ, a peerless interpreter of the mind of Jesus. Now he defended and proclaimed as Lord

"Saul must have had something happen to him . . . he's not even keeping score anymore."

the very same one whom he had persecuted so strongly and fiercely.

He had a poor beginning. Yet look what happened. A poor beginning can be redeemed.

The Importance of a Good Beginning

So the beginning is important. True, it isn't everything — a good one can be wasted; a poor one can be overcome. But while the beginning isn't everything, let us stress that it is very important. As it is in golf, so it is in life: the significance of a good drive, or a fine start, cannot be over-emphasized.

1. A good beginning is vital for your Christian life. Some of you are new Christians. You haven't been a disciple for very long. It means so much for you to get off to a good start.

Or if you have been neglecting your Christian life, now is the time to start anew. Perhaps you have become careless and unconcerned about following Jesus. It is never too late to start over again.

You need to study the Word. The Bible is your guidebook, your source of power and inspiration. Are you well acquainted with it? Do you turn to it regularly, daily? Are you growing in your knowledge of it?

You need to develop your devotional life. Is some part of every day reserved for the Lord? Is this time sacred? Is your prayer life increasing? Is your personal fellowship with the Lord deepening each day?

You need to understand your own faith, to know what Christianity is all about. What do you believe? And why? Are you able to give a reason for the faith that is within you? Is the Christian Gospel more reasonable, more logical, more meaningful today than it was last month?

You need also to learn how to witness, to share your faith.

How often do you invite a friend or a neighbor to come with you to worship? How long has it been since you introduced someone to Jesus, the Savior? How natural is it for you to talk about spiritual matters and encourage others to enjoy the abundant life?

2. A good beginning is vital for a young life. Children are so important. They are gifts from God, and we who are parents are responsible for the diligent training of each child entrusted to us. And there is no substitute for those first, early years of a child's life. Then is the time to set the proper direction of each new life and pour the desirable values into it.

A short time ago, I was talking with a young mother. She was telling of a recent experience. Her son had a playmate who lived three houses down the street. One day, while the boys were playing in the yard, she asked her son's friend, "Where do you go to Sunday school?"

He did not seem to quite understand. So she explained, "Where do you go to learn about Jesus?"

His reply stunned her, "Who's Jesus?"

"Who's Jesus?" He had never heard. Almost six years old. And knew nothing about Jesus! So she told him, there in the backyard, some stories about Jesus. And he listened. With eyes wide open. With ears wide open. With heart wide open. Eagerly. Drinking in the truth of Jesus.

What had this boy's parents done to him? They had cheated him. They had not even used Christmas as a chance to talk about Jesus — and it is his birthday. Those parents, I learned later, were members of a church. But how negligent they were. They had deprived their son of a good beginning.

3. A good beginning is vital for every day. When you wake up in the morning, what is the first thing you do? Why not just say a prayer? Lift up your thoughts, the very first moment of

each day, to the highest, the best, the noblest that you know. As you wake, give the day to God; commend it to his keeping; ask him to use it; turn it over to him. Bishop Ralph S. Cushman's fine piece of poetry stresses the value of a good beginning each day:

I met God in the morning
When the day was at its best,
And his Presence came like sunrise,
Like a glory in my breast.

All day long the Presence lingered,
All day long he stayed with me,
And we sailed in perfect calmness
O'er a very troubled sea.

Other ships were blown and battered,
Other ships were sore distressed,
But the winds that seemed to drive them
Brought to us a peace and rest.

Then I thought of other mornings,
With a keen remorse of mind,
When I too had loosed the moorings
With the Presence left behind.

So I think I know the secret,
Learned from many a troubled way:
You must seek him in the morning
If you want him through the day!

2

"Down the Fairway"

Chapter Two

Once you drive a golf ball off the tee, you have not completed your job. Most of the time, when playing a hole of golf, you still have to hit the ball a second or a third time (or more!) before you reach the green, which is your destination. This means that, though your drive may have been a beautiful one, though it may have been the longest and straightest drive in the world, still you have to continue down the fairway.

And those next shots down the fairway are, in some ways, even more demanding than the drive off the tee. For as you get closer to the green, you must be even more accurate. You just do not dare to drift very far to one side or the other. If you stray very far, you are apt to be in the woods, in the rough, in the sand, in the water — in trouble of some kind — and it may cost you additional strokes.

A golf story comes to mind; it illustrates what I have in mind.

A golfer hit his ball from the tee and it looked as if the ball were going straight down the fairway. But it soon began to bend and sliced off to the right, coming to rest at the very edge of the fairway — under a tree, nestled quietly between two large ant hills. When the golfer arrived and saw where his ball was, he carefully selected a club for his next shot down the fairway. He wound up and took a mighty swing. The sand flew in every direction, but there lay the ball — it had not moved at all. One of the ant hills had been demolished and the ants were scurrying everywhere. But the ball was untouched.

Well, of course it was the fault of the club, so the golfer put the club back into his bag, chose another, took his stance, and made another prodigious swing. Once again, the sand flew in every direction. Once again, the ball did not move. This time, the other ant hill had been destroyed; the ants were racing in all directions — and the ball remained in place.

As the golfer paused for a moment of silent meditation, he heard a still, small voice. It was one of the ants calling to the others, "Hey, if we want to be safe, we'd better get on the ball."

Now this is true in life . . . if we want to be safe, we need to get on the ball. And this is true in church and in Christianity . . . if we want to be safe, we need to get on the ball for Jesus Christ. We need to be on the ball — for him. And this means going down the straight and narrow fairway.

Two Ways of Life

Most of us remember these words of Jesus, from the Sermon on the Mount: "Enter by the narrow gate; for the gate is wide and the way is easy that leads to destruction, and those who enter by it are many. For the gate is narrow and the way is hard that leads to life, and those who find it are few." (Matthew 7:13, 14)

It is easy to see how this applies to golf. Broad and wide is the way that leads into the woods — and lots of golfers find it. How well I know.

Straight and narrow is the way that leads to the green, and

those who find it are few — at least, on the first try.

As you go down the fairway, no matter what kind of start you have had, accuracy is at a premium. The closer you get to the green, the narrower your margin for error becomes.

This is true in golf, and this is true in life. Wide and broad and open is the fairway of life that leads into trouble, trouble of all kinds. Straight and narrow is the fairway of life that leads to that which is good, worthwhile, and eternal. And we each decide which route we will travel.

In the first Psalm, there is a sharp contrast between two ways of life. "For the Lord knows the *way of the righteous,* but the *way of the wicked* will perish." (Psalm 1:6) One way is the antithesis of the other.

And as you read through that Psalm (indeed, as you read through the entire Bible) you find this contrast: **A WAY** of life against **THE WAY** of life.

There is **A WAY** of life — a way of life that is false, wide, and broad. It leads to trouble and destruction. The Bible talks about it in this manner, "There is **A WAY** which seems right to a man, but its end is the way to death." (Proverbs 14:12; 16:25)

Opposed to **A WAY** of life, however, is **THE WAY** of life — the way of life which is straight, true, and narrow. It leads into the fullness of life. The Bible talks about it in this manner, "This is **THE WAY;** walk in it." (Isaiah 30:21)

Note the contrast of these two quotations. "There is **A WAY** which seems right to a man, but its end is the way to death." "This is **THE WAY;** walk in it."

Then Jesus, when he came, added a personal note by saying, "I am **THE WAY** . . . he who follows me will not walk in darkness, but will have the light of life." (John 14:6; 8:12) He calls himself **THE WAY.**

So the first Psalm is, in a sense, a miniature of the whole Bible. It presents the stark contrast: **A WAY** vs. **THE WAY.**

A WAY, which seems right and is easy to follow, but which leads only to trouble. Or **THE WAY,** which is harder to find and more difficult to walk, but which leads to life.

And you make the choice, each of you, individually. Which will it be? Will you follow **A WAY** — or **THE WAY?** Will you follow the false, wide, broad way that leads to destruction? Or the straight, narrow, true way that leads to fullness and abundance of life? Will you listen to your own inclinations and learn, "There is **A WAY** which seems right to a man, but its end is the way to death"? Or will you listen to the words of Scripture as they teach you, "This is **THE WAY;** walk in it"? Or "Jesus is **THE WAY** — walk in him"?

The Way of Resurrection

The Gospel according to St. Luke is a beautiful account that abounds in stories from the life of Jesus — stories that he lived, and also stories that he told. Luke relates many incidents and parables we do not find in any of the other Gospels. If it were not for Luke, there would be many now-familiar stories missing. Let me call your attention to three of these stories from Luke, in order to illustrate our central point.

The first is the story of the prodigal son (Luke 15:11-32). Only Luke tells this story. We all know the parable. The younger of two sons went to his father and asked for his inheritance. Finally he received it.

Off he went into a far country. He wasted his life. He squandered his money. He threw it away in what he thought was a wild and glorious time.

And then came — well, today we would call it a recession. The bottom dropped out. His money was gone. His friends left — because they were the kind of friends who can be bought only with money. There were no jobs. He found himself alone, destitute, and hungry.

"Why am I doing this anyway? Back home my dad owns an entire golf course!"

Finally the boy sank so low that he was out in the fields feeding the pigs. Now that is about as low as a Jewish boy can fall (remember the Hebrew attitude toward pigs). And there this boy was — hungry enough to eat the garbage he was feeding to the swine.

But there in the pigpen, he came to himself. He came to his senses. He realized what a stupid fool he'd been, how ridiculous his way of life had been. He made up his mind to go back home and ask his dad to allow him to be just a hired servant.

I suggest that it was a long, hard, painful trip for that prodigal to make, as he walked back home. It is not easy to admit your mistakes. It is not easy to return to your father's house with nothing — nothing except a confession of sin on your lips. It's a narrow, straight, difficult way.

But it's the way that leads to resurrection. Remember what the father said when he welcomed his son, "This my son was dead, and is alive again." The boy had been dead — dead in his trespasses and his sins (Ephesians 2:1,5; Colossians 2:13). Now he was alive again — reborn into newness of life — because he took that long, difficult, painful way. It was the way of resurrection.

The Way of Forgiveness

Here is another story recorded only by Luke. Jesus had been invited into the home of a Pharisee, a man named Simon (Luke 7:36-50). Simon had also invited some of the social leaders of the community. Together they were reclining in the courtyard, enjoying their meal.

To the amazement of everyone, from the street into the courtyard came a woman of the world. She made her way over to Jesus. She knelt at his feet. Tears were flowing freely down her cheeks and dropping on his feet. Literally, she washed his feet with her tears and dried them with her long hair. Then she took out a small bottle of precious ointment and anointed the feet of Jesus.

Without telling the rest of the story (be sure to read it for yourself) I suggest that this was no easy thing for that woman to do. It was a narrow, straight, agonizing way for her — to kneel at the feet of Jesus. It was a difficult, painful step to take — to openly acknowledge her sin in the presence of the respected community leaders.

It was not an easy way. But it was the way of forgiveness. Before she left that courtyard, she heard Jesus say, "Your sins are forgiven."

The Way of Justification

Another story told by Jesus and reported only by St. Luke is found in chapter 18 (Luke 18:9-14). Jesus tells of two men who went up to the temple. They wanted to pray. One was a Pharisee; the other, a publican. The Pharisee, a religious ruler. The publican, a despised tax collector.

The Pharisee raised his hands, lifted his eyes, and said, "God, I thank thee that I am not like other men."

Then he went on to tell God just how good he was: "I tithe, I fast. I serve on many boards and committees. I was elected a trustee. I give $100 a week in the offering." I realize, I am elaborating on the Scriptures, but essentially that is what he was saying. "O God, I'm glad I'm better than other men."

The tax collector was different. The publican, not daring to lift up his eyes to heaven, but dropping his head on his chest and smiting himself upon his breast, cried out, "God, be merciful to me, a sinner!"

It is never easy, even in private, let alone in a public place, to admit to a holy God your frailties, your weaknesses, your mistakes, your shortcomings. I suggest that what the publican

"Lord, I thank you I am not like other golfers . . ."

did that day in the temple was not easy. It was a narrow, hurtful, lonely way that he walked. But it was the way of justification. For he walked into the presence of the righteous Lord, in all his majesty and glory. And Jesus said of that publican, "He went down to his house justified rather than the other."

Walking In *THE WAY*

The way to life is a long, difficult, painful way. But the prodigal found it was the way of resurrection; the sinful woman found it was the way of forgiveness; and the publican found it was the way of justification.

Just as the way of resurrection, of forgiveness, and of justification is a straight and narrow way, so is the way we are called upon to walk after we give our lives to the Lord, after we trust in him. Those who are loved are expected to be loving. Those who are forgiven are expected to be forgiving. Those who find compassion and understanding are expected to be compassionate and understanding.

We all know the story — we hear it repeatedly, and always it continues to haunt and challenge us — of the Savior who, with nails piercing his hands, said, "Father, forgive them for they know not what they do." (Luke 23:34)

We recall the story of Jesus telling Peter, "Seventy times seven." (Matthew 18:21, 22). That is how often you should be willing to forgive your brother.

Do you remember what you pray when you say the Lord's Prayer? "Forgive us our trespasses, *as we forgive* those who trespass against us." Do you really want God to forgive you to the same extent that you are willing to forgive others? That is what you ask. If you do not mean that, you had better be careful about praying the Lord's Prayer.

It is possible to live this way. An old story, from a rural community, illustrates. Farmer Smith and Farmer Brown were neighbors. One day Farmer Smith found Farmer Brown's cows in his cornfield. The fence had broken and the cows went through. He took them down to the public authorities, and wrote Farmer Brown a note. It read, "Your cows broke into my cornfield. I found them and took them to the authorities. If they do it again, I'll do the same thing."

A few weeks later, the circumstances were reversed. Farmer Brown found Farmer Smith's cows in his cornfield. Brown put them back, repaired the fence, and sent a note to Farmer Smith: "Your cows broke into my cornfield. I put them back and repaired the fence. If they do it again, I'll do the same thing."

That is **THE WAY** of life. And that is ***THE* WAY** of Jesus. And that is **THE WAY** we need to learn io walk. For as we receive the mercy of God, so we should share the mercy of God. As we receive the grace of God, so we should share the grace of God. As we receive the love of God, so we should share the love of God.

One of my favorite stories is of the mother who went to Napoleon. Her son was in Napoleon's army. He had been arrested, tried, and sentenced to execution. She went to plead for his life. At length, she was ushered into the presence of the Emperor, Napoleon himself. She pleaded for her son. Napoleon said, "But this is his second offense. Justice demands that he die."

"But," she replied, "I'm not asking for justice. I'm pleading for mercy."

"But he doesn't deserve mercy."

"Please, sir, if he deserved it, it wouldn't be mercy."

And the story relates that Napoleon was so touched and so impressed that the woman's son was set free.

And this is a picture of us before the infinite God. We do not deserve his mercy, his grace, his forgiveness. It has been freely bestowed upon us, unworthy though we are.

Now we, in turn, need to offer that same kind of grace and

mercy, love and forgiveness, to others — whether or not they deserve it.

"Enter by the narrow gate; for the gate is wide and the way is easy that leads to destruction, and those who enter by it are many. For the gate is narrow and the way is hard that leads to life, and those who find it are few."

3

Fore!

Chapter Three

Everyone who goes golfing knows what the word "Fore" — F, O, R, E — means. It is a shout of warning, a signal of impending danger.

If you happen to be on or near a golf course and you hear somebody yell, "Fore!" the thing to do is duck first and ask questions afterward. Because this cry means that a golf ball might be coming into your vicinity. And this can be threatening.

When golfers get on the course and hit the ball, it does not always go where they intend. If it did, of course, they would always score a hole-in-one, or at least a birdie. Unfortunately, the ball frequently goes off target, sometimes right in the direction of someone who is completely unsuspecting. To warn these people, the word, "Fore," is yelled. It means, "Watch out! Be careful!"

When I am golfing and hear somebody shout, "Fore!", the first thing I do is drop to my hands and knees and cover my head with my arms. Later, I can look around and see whether he meant me. Because a golf ball, hit with a swinging club, can be a dangerous missile.

Last year over 10,000 people were struck with golf balls. And those are just the ones who were reported; only the Lord himself knows how many more are unreported.

In the twelfth chapter of the book of the Gospel as it has been recorded by St. Luke, there are at least three places where Jesus shouts, "Fore!" He does not use *that* word. But he does call out a word of warning. He wants to alert his followers to menacing dangers. He wants to warn us. He wants to protect us. He wants us to be careful. Those three cries are what I wish to call to your attention.

Beware of Hypocrisy

In the very first verse, this is what Jesus says: "Beware of the leaven of the Pharisees, which is hypocrisy." (Luke 12:1) "Beware," he tells us, "beware of hypocrisy."

Each of us has some idea of what this means. The Greek word which is translated "hypocrisy" simply means "to play a part." A hypocrite is someone who plays a part. An actor or an actress. That, literally, is the original meaning of the word.

An actor goes on stage and plays a part. He is not really the person he portrays; he is only acting, playing a part. Of course, for a period of time, he does everything possible to put himself into his role; he tries to become that person as much as he can. But actually, he is not really that person. He is playing a part. He is, in the Greek language, a hypocrite.

The word "hypocrite" today has come to mean anybody who professes to be something that he or she really is not. In all of life, not just on a stage. There are many people in the drama of life who are simply actors — pretending to be something that they are not.

Generally, the word is used to describe a worldly person who pretends to be a Christian. One who goes through the motions, attends and supports the church, participates in the rituals and ceremonies, puts up a good front, and makes others believe that he is better than he really is. A worldly person who seeks to deceive others into thinking he is a devoted Christian. That is one kind of hypocrite.

There are other kinds. Indeed, the very opposite is true. There are also hypocrites who are Christians pretending to be worldly. They do want to be the best, the cleanest, and the noblest they can be.

Yet when they are in their everyday world, with their friends, neighbors, and fellow-workers, they just go along and acquiesce with the worldly life around them. It is so easy for them to go along with some of the vulgar habits and attitudes of the world round about them. It is so easy for them to listen to the off-color jokes. It is so easy for them to listen to the filthy language, even to allow their own to become a bit tainted. They hesitate to object. They find it difficult to speak up, to take a stand, to try to be true to the highest and the purest they know. They do not want to subject themselves to possible ridicule or mockery.

There are Christians who pretend to go along with the people with whom they work, Christians who accommodate themselves to their daily life, Christians who pretend to be "one of the guys." But it makes them uncomfortable. Deep down inside, they are not really people of the world. This is another form of hypocrisy.

Jesus says, "Beware of hypocrisy." Beware of any kind of pretending. Let's be ourselves. Let's be who we are. And then let's be what God intends us to be.

The Pharisee is the chief example that Jesus uses of hypocrisy — in this chapter and in many other passages. He says, "Beware of the leaven of the Pharisees, which is hypocrisy." Again Jesus said, "Woe to you, scribes and Pharisees, hypocrites." (Matthew 23:13, 14, 15, 23, 25, 27, 29) The Pharisees were the religious leaders of that day. No one could accuse them of not being religious; they were very religious people. No one could accuse them of not being sincere; they were very sincere people.

But the Pharisee was one who emphasized the little things about religion, and neglected many of the vital and important things. He stressed minor and insignificant details, but missed some of the values that are really central and eternal.

Jesus used the illustration of the speck and the log in a person's eye (Matthew 7:3-5). To freely translate, this is what he said, "You Pharisees are just like a person who tries to take a little piece of dirt out of someone else's eye. It's a tiny speck; it's very difficult to locate; and you're deeply concerned that it be removed. In the meantime, what is in your own eye? A two-by-four! Here you are, looking for a speck of dust in another person's eye, while you have a whole plank in your own eye!"

Now Jesus was exaggerating, of course. That's how he made his point. It is ridiculous to think of a person with a two-by-four in his eye. This demonstrates the sense of humor Jesus had. This exaggeration drives home his idea — that the Pharisees stressed the trivial matters of religion and overlooked the great elements of faith and justice, of righteousness and holiness.

Jesus uses another illustration, and it has an element of humor as well. He talks about "straining a gnat and swallowing a camel." (Matthew 23:24) Can you imagine that? You take your drinking water and strain it — to remove all the bugs, flies, and gnats. You want it to be clean and pure. Then you turn right around and drink a camel! Of course it is silly to think of someone having a camel going down his throat. But again, the exaggeration and the humor make plain the truth: that the Pharisees were so obsessed with the rites and customs, the rituals and ceremonies (the minor elements of religion) that they neglected justice, purity, and holiness (the major elements of religion).

We still have our Pharisees — those who can make long

"I am not 'straining at gnats'. I just don't think you should let him count that hole-in-one, the way the wind was blowing in his favor."

prayers, who pay very careful attention to every little detail of the church service, and who administer a church very strictly. Then, like the Pharisees, they can go right out and cheat a poor widow out of her inheritance, overcharge for an inferior piece of merchandise — or something else equally bad. We have those today who emphasize the trivial and evade the essential.

"Beware of hypocrisy," said Jesus. Don't try to pretend; don't try to play a part. You may be able to fool other people. You may be able to fool the preacher (that's no great achievement). You may even be able to fool yourself. But you simply cannot fool God. You cannot pretend with him. He knows for certain what you really are.

One of the historic prayers of the church begins, "Almighty God, unto whom all hearts are open, all desires known, and from whom no secrets are hid . . . "

And Jesus, in this chapter adds, "Nothing is covered up that will not be revealed, or hidden that will not be known." (Luke 12:2).

Beware of Satan

A little farther in the chapter, Jesus continues, "Do not fear those who kill the body, and after that have no more that they can do. But I will warn you whom to fear: fear him who, after he has killed, has power to cast into hell" (Luke 12:4, 5).

Now there are many questions of interpretation about this verse. Some commentators believe it refers to God. Others think it refers to Satan. The translations and the controversies are matters for the scholars. But I take this passage to mean just what it says. My opinion: the reference is to Satan. He is the one who casts into hell.

God never sends anybody to hell. Anyone who goes to hell goes there in spite of God, not because of him. God wants to deliver us from the power of evil. He wants to free us. To this end, he sent his only Son, our Lord Jesus, the Savior. When we go to hell, it is because we choose to go, because we defy God, not because he sends us. God is "not wishing that any should perish, but that all should reach repentance." (2 Peter 3:9).

So Jesus is saying here, "Beware of Satan." And this is still good advice — "Beware of the devil."

I believe in the devil. Our modern generation does not. We have relegated him to the back burner, kept him pretty much out of sight, and taught that he is merely a symbol, a figure of speech, a myth, a legend. He may be all of these, but he is more. To me, Satan is a reality. To Jesus, Satan was a reality. In the New Testament, Satan is a reality.

Jesus tells the parable, in Matthew 13, about a farmer who went out to sow his seed. Then a little later, somebody else came and sowed some tares, some weeds, right in with all the good seed. Everything grew up together. When the servants saw it, they went to the master and asked, "What's happening here?" His explanation, "An enemy has done this." And Jesus, when he explained the meaning of that parable to his disciples, said, "The enemy who sowed them is the devil." (Matthew 13:39)

The devil is still busy sowing tares where the Lord has already sown the good seed — in your heart, and in mine.

Another time, speaking to a group of wicked Jewish people, Jesus said to them, "You are of your father the devil." (John 8:44) His meaning is clear: "You're not God's children; you're the devil's children." A mere figure of speech?

On the night of the Last Supper, the Bible tells us that "Satan entered into Judas." (John 13:27; Luke 22:3) Just a figure of speech?

Here in this chapter (Luke 12), Jesus urges us to beware of Satan. Would Jesus tell us to beware of a myth? Or to beware of a legend? Was the devil a figure of speech to Adam and Eve in the Garden of Eden? Was the devil a figure of speech

"The devil made me do it."

to Job in the midst of his trials and tribulations? Was the devil a figure of speech to Jesus out in the wilderness during his temptation encounter?

One of the most effective devices Satan has ever found is to get us to doubt his existence. If we do not believe that he is real, then he's got it made! He has us where he wants us.

Suppose you were to go out of church, or leave your home, and met a creature with horns, a bright red suit, a long tail, pointed pitchfork, and all. Suppose he came up to you and said, "Come on, come along with me; I want to take you down the street. I've got something wonderful for you." How much temptation would that be? It would be no problem at all to kick such a being in the seat of his red pants and send him on his way. There would be no temptation to follow him.

But that is not the way the devil operates. The New Testament says he "disguises himself as an angel of light." (2 Corinthians 11:14) He can take that which is wicked and transform it into something appealing. He makes sin so alluring and attractive that you can hardly turn away. Ha takes evil and makes it glitter, so as to be irresistible. He entices us, with beauty. He seduces us, with loveliness. How magnetically and how effectively he has learned to work in the hearts of men. No wonder Jesus says, "Beware of Satan."

Beware of Covetousness

Then a bit later in the chapter, Jesus says, "Take heed, and beware of covetousness" (Luke 12:15). Isn't that interesting? Three times within a few verses, Jesus says that we should beware. First, "Beware of hypocrisy." Then, "Beware of Satan." And now, "Beware of covetousness."

"Take heed, and beware of covetousness, for a man's life does not consist in the abundance of his possessions."

By covetousness Jesus means materialism. Materialism —

becoming so obsessed with the things of this world that we lose sight of the fact there are some other values infinitely more important. This is pertinent for today. Jesus wants all of us to examine ourselves, because we too are in danger of yielding to this very temptation.

Not very many of us are covetous in the sense that we are out to accumulate all we can get at the expense of other people. But we are covetous in the sense that we have become so concerned about this life that we tend to forget the next, so concerned with time that we forget eternity, so concerned with the physical that we forget the spiritual.

What occupies most of our time, attention, and energy? What do we really want from life? A beautiful home, lovely furniture, the best food, ability to pay the bills, a bit of a surplus in the bank account or the money market?

These are the material things of life. And a multitude of Americans live this way — desiring these materialistic possessions. The family across the street buys a new car. Why can't we have a new car? The people next door have an Atari computer. Why can't we have one, too?

Now it isn't wrong to be materialistic. It isn't sinful to want a nice house. It isn't wicked to want "the good things of life." It isn't immoral to drive an automobile, have enough food, and pay our bills.

The sin lies in becoming so engrossed with these things that nothing else really matters. The eternal ideals are forgotten. The spiritual values are neglected. This is the danger of our generation today. Not simply that we are materialistic, but that we are only materialistic.

You see, Jesus did not say, "Man does not live by bread." We do. We do live by bread. But Jesus did say, "Man shall not live by bread *alone*." (Matthew 4:4)

There is something more to a person than the physical. And this is the part that Jesus says is vital, the part that is eternal, the part that lives forever — not simply for three score and ten years.

How often we become so concerned about the material things of life — with making a living, with obtaining a supply of money, with doing the best we can for our family and loved ones — that we lose sight of the fact that we have souls as well as bodies.

In this very chapter, Jesus uses a good illustration (Luke 12:16-21). He told of the rich fool, a wealthy farmer who apparently had everything that life had to offer. He was independent, prosperous, respected, self-reliant — an outstanding success.

And he thought within himself, "What will I do? I don't even have room enough to store all my goods. My barns aren't big enough. This is what I'll do. I will pull down the old barns and I'll build bigger ones. I'll build barns that are big enough to take care of all I have. And I'll put all my fruits and my goods into these new, large barns. And then I will say to my soul, 'Soul, You have ample goods laid up for many years . . .' "

Oh no, wait a minute! He was wrong. He was not talking to his soul. What he was really saying was, "Body, you have ample goods laid up for many years. Take your ease. Eat, drink, and be merry." He was talking to his body, not to his soul. He was concerned only for his physical welfare. He ignored his eternal, spiritual welfare.

This is the danger that our generation faces today — the danger of materialism, of greed, of covetousness. "Take heed, and beware of covetousness, for a man's life does not consist in the abundance of his possessions."

On a golf course, when a golfer shouts, "Fore!", he is trying to help you. He does not want you to get hurt. He is shouting to warn you.

In the New Testament when Jesus shouts, "Beware!", it is

"Me? Jealous of Jake? No way!"

the same. He is doing it to help us. He is warning us. He wants us to avoid these dangers.

"Beware of hypocrisy." "Beware of Satan." "Beware of covetousness."

4

"In A Hazard"

Chapter Four

The game of golf, in many ways, can be compared to the game of life. And those of you who are golfers are aware that between the beginning of a golf hole (driving off the tee) and the conclusion (where you finally putt the ball into the cup), between the tee and the green, we face various hazards, or obstacles.

There is the rough — high grass, trees, and woods. There is the water — lakes, creeks, and ponds. There are bunkers — sand traps and mounds. And it always seems that they happen to be just at the right (or the wrong) place. They always seem to be where we do not want them to be. Or, more truthfully, we find ourselves where we do not really wish to be.

I could tell many stories about obstacles and hazards. This one comes to mind. I was golfing with one of the men of our church and had made a miserable start. I was very frustrated and disgusted.

Then we came to the Number five hole, a short par three, which is right across a lake. I drove off the tee, and — plop!

Into the water went the ball. My former district superintendent would say that it had been baptized.

So I teed up another ball and swung again. Plop! Into the water. I teed up a third ball — and three in a row had dropped into the water!

Finally I grabbed my cart and, angry and upset at myself, rushed around the lake. As I started up a sloping hill toward the green, the cart overturned and all the clubs went sprawling on the grass alongside the water. I turned to my partner and exclaimed, "Good night! I can't even pull a cart right today!"

Right then, I was tempted to throw the cart, the bag, the clubs, right into the lake and give up golf forever.

And sometimes in life, we have days like that. Everything seems to go wrong. We feel like running away and hiding; we think we ought to give up and quit. The hazards of life seem to crush and shatter us.

Not By Choice

It is important to remember that a golfer is never in a hazard by choice. We do not deliberately or intentionally enter these hazards. Golfers do not go into a sand trap because they like to play with sand or build sand castles. They do not go into the woods because they think it is cool and shady there.

There is no temptation to get into the traps or the woods or the other hazards. There is nothing appealing, there is nothing alluring about them at all.

Golfers try to avoid the hazards of a course if they can. And yet, we enter those hazards in spite of our best intentions.

Life is like that. We find ourselves in situations which do not happen by choice, that we prefer to steer clear of. Circumstances often force us into a hazard of life, whether or not we like it, whether or not we desire it.

Disappointments, frustrations, accidents, tragedies, loss of health, loss of business, loss of income, an overload of debt, sickness, hospitalization, serious surgery, an unfaithful spouse, a severe handicap: these are some of the conditions that stand in our way, conditions over which we have no control. We did our best to avoid them. There was nothing tempting about them. But they happened anyhow. We find ourselves in distressing predicaments in spite of our best efforts.

Be An Overcomer

The mark of a good golfer is not whether or not he gets into the hazards. The best of golfers get into the hazards — Jack Nicklaus, Arnold Palmer, Tom Watson. They all know what it's like to be in the sand, in the rough, in the trees, in the water.

So the mark of a good golfer is not whether or not he eludes the obstacles; the mark of a good golfer is that he does not quit. When he gets into an unwanted hazard, he does not give up.

The good golfer knows how to recover. It amazes me, when I watch the professionals on television, to see how they can intentionally hook the ball around some trees and land on the green. Or splash the ball from shallow water on to the green. Or go into a sand trap and blast the ball to within inches of the flag — or even hole it out. Hazards do not bother them. They recover; they overcome.

Now the duffer knows what needs to be done, but unfortunately he does not get it done. Often we go into a sand trap, for instance, disgusted with ourselves for getting there in the first place. Then we take a half-hearted swing, spray the sand everywhere, and hardly move the ball a foot or two. Thus, in our half-heartedness and frustration, we add strokes to our score.

When you find yourself in a hazard of life, take the professional way out. When you are threatened or overwhelmed by the hazards of life, learn how to recover. Don't give up; don't quit; don't rebel; don't pout; don't complain. And don't forsake God. He still loves you; he still wants to redeem you. Life can still be useful; you can still get a good score out of it. You can still recover. Be an overcomer, not a duffer.

Jesus put it a different way. He said, "In the world, ye shall have tribulation."

But he did not stop there; he continued, "But be of good cheer, I have overcome the world." (John 16:33)

And the implication is that we too, in the game of life, will have tribulation. We cannot escape it. But we also, through our faith in Jesus, can overcome the world. This is the essence of the message for us: we can be overcomers.

Mark

Here are a couple biblical illustrations. In the New Testament, there is young man named Mark — John Mark. Young Mark traveled with Paul and Barnabas on their first missionary journey, the one that begins in the thirteenth chapter of Acts.

He went along as a helper. Then at one point in the journey, at Perga, he turned back and went home (Acta 13:13). We don't know why. Didn't he like it? Did he get homesick? Did he become tired of the work? Or was there an argument? We don't really know what happened.

But whatever the reason, he did not finish his job. Paul and Barnabas carried on by themselves. They finished the trip and returned to Antioch.

Several months later they decided it was time for another journey. Barnabas, who was the uncle of young Mark (Colossians 4:10), said to Paul, "We'll take Mark with us again."

And Paul answered, "Nothing doing. No way. He left us once. That's it. I've had it with him."

Because of their conflict over young Mark, who had deserted them on the first journey, Paul and Barnabas actually split up. Their argument was that serious. Their dissension led to

"Come on, John Mark, let's give it one more try."

separation (Acts 15:36-40).

Without going into all the details, we may conclude that Mark may have been a deserter, Mark may have left the job, Mark may not have finished what he started — but Mark overcame his faults, his shortcomings.

Sometime later he became a companion of Peter. And in his epistle, Peter calls Mark his son in the faith (1 Peter 5:13).

Even Paul himself, who had argued so strongly against Mark, later realized that Mark had overcome his handicap, and he called Mark "very useful in serving me." (2 Timothy 4:11)

Mark went on to become the author of one of our four biblical accounts of the life of Jesus — the Gospel according to Saint Mark. *Saint* Mark! No one would have expected this!

Mark was an overcomer. He did not allow his mistakes, his failures to get him down. He kept at it. And still made something of himself, by the grace of God.

Hosea

There is a man in the Old Testament who teaches a similar lesson. His name is Hosea. We know him as a great prophet.

Hosea had a wife who deserted him. Her name was Gomer. She simply turned her back on Hosea and their three children. She just ran away and went out into a life of sin and adultery (Hosea 2:5). Hosea was heartbroken, crushed.

At length, his wife reached the bottom. One day as he walked through the marketplace, he passed the auction block, where slaves were being sold. He looked up. And then turned around. There was his wife! Being sold to the highest bidder, as a slave.

What did Hosea do? He realized that he still loved Gomer. No matter what had happened, no matter what she had done. He still knew a deep, heartfelt love. He bought her! He redeemed her! He restored her into his home! (Hosea 3:2).

This experience provides the basis for the emphasis of the prophet Hosea. He reasoned like this: if a human being can love this way, in spite of sin and degradation, how much more the divine Creator. If a mere husband can love a wayward wife this much, how much more the heavenly Father must love his wandering children, whatever they have done. And the whole message of the prophet Hosea is a message of love, as he calls upon an unfaithful Israel to return to her God, a God who still loves and still cares.

Joseph

Remember the story of Joseph, back in the Old Testament. He was a dreamer. His brothers did not like his dreams. They hated young Joseph.

Then one time they caught him away from home and dropped him into a pit, intending to kill him. But one brother had a touch of compassion, so they dragged him out of the pit and, instead of killing him, sold him to a traveling band of merchants.

He was taken down into the land of Egypt. There he became a slave. He became such a good slave that his master placed him in charge of the rest of the slaves.

Then he was tempted by his master's wife, but resisted her seduction. Because of his purity, he was then thrown into prison. For being good! For being virtuous!

He spent two years in prison. He was completely forgotten by the butler, who had promised that he would tell Pharaoh about Joseph.

One affliction after another; one ordeal after another; one adversity after another. One hazard after another. But Joseph never gave up. Ultimately, he became the prime minister of Egypt, second only to the Pharaoh. (These familiar stories are found in Genesis 37-41). And he became the great forgiver —

"My husband will be on the links all day. Suppose the two of us . . ."

probably the person in the Old Testament who is closest to Jesus in love, compassion, and forgiveness (Genesis 45).

Harry H______

Mark was an overcomer. Hosea was an overcomer. Joseph was an overcomer. The following account tells of a twentieth century overcomer, a man named Harry H______, from New York state, a man who had all kinds of obstacles in his early life.

He became a high school teacher, which was his goal — in spite of the fact that he himself had been a dropout from school; in spite of the fact that his father had lost his business; in spite of the fact that he had served overseas in the Army; and in spite of the fact that by the time he finally got to college and trained to be a high school teacher, he was married and had a family to care for. But he achieved his goal.

Then, to demonstrate how the hazards pile up, he developed serious trouble with his back and spinal column. He underwent seven serious operations over a period of several years, enduring excruciating pain all the time. Agony, torture, anguish — constantly.

The only answer was drugs. He took so many drugs that he became addicted. As many as fifteen to twenty doctors, over a wide area, were providing him with prescriptions. He reached the verge of suicide.

Finally one day, Harry and his wife, a registered nurse, sat down and determined to lick that habit. They did.

Not many of us know about it first-hand, but it is a terrible thing to break the drug habit. All night: sweat, cramps, nausea, fever, diarrhea, his body shrieking for drugs.

It was a tremendous struggle. But they overcame. Long days of suspense and dread followed. After three months, life settled back to normal again.

Then one day after school, a couple detectives stopped him.

A spot check had revealed his addiction. He was taken into court, found guilty, and sentenced to a six-month term.

There in prison, he was amazed at the number of teen-agers, young people just like those he had been teaching back in the high school classroom.

They didn't have anything to do — they just sat around, bragged about their crimes, and started fights. He went to the warden. The warden and the sheriff cooperated, and he started a class behind bars.

Out of that first class, four young boys returned to school after they left prison. Another, who had been considered incorrigible, started his own business. And many other youth in the class found that they had a particular aptitude for mathematics, or science, or language. It was amazing what he uncovered.

The outcome of the story is that when Harry himself was released, he was employed as a teacher-director, to institute this kind of program in as many prisons as possible.[1] Harry is an overcomer.

My point is simply this: you too can be an overcomer.

The words of the Scriptures are not merely words. The eighth chapter of Romans is the eternal truth. Listen again. "We know that in everything (everything — failure, weaknesses, mistakes, sin, death, sickness) God works for good with those who love him . . . What then shall we say to this (these hazards that overwhelm us)? If God is for us, who is against us? . . . Who shall separate us from the love of Christ? Shall tribulation, or distress, or persecution, or famine, or nakedness, or peril, or sword? . . . No, in all these things we are *more than conquerors* through him who loved us. For I am sure that neither death, nor life, nor angels, nor principalities, nor powers, nor things present, nor things to come, nor height, nor depth, nor

---

This true story is told in *Good Housekeeping*, (September, 1960) and is summarized by permission.

anything else in all creation will be able to separate us from the love of God in Christ Jesus our Lord!" Romans 8:28, 31, 35, 37, 38, 39) You too can be an overcomer.

5

"ON THE GREEN"

Chapter Five

We have been comparing the game of golf to the game of life. Now we are on the green. We have arrived. This is the goal we have been seeking. All the way from the tee, down the fairway, through the hazards — this has been our target.

When you drive by a golf course, the green catches your eye immediately. It's that smoothly cut, velvety rich, bright green grass that stands out and attracts you right away. To draw your attention even more toward the green, there is usually a flag waving on it. That colorful, vivid area is the goal of every golfer.

But even when you reach the green, you still have not finished. You still must putt out. You have to hit the ball up close to the flag, then into the hole. A hole of golf is not finished till the ball is actually in the cup.

The average golfer, when he reaches the green, has a temptation to become complacent and relaxed. Often he thinks, deep inside his heart, "Whew, at last, now I've finally got it made." As a result, he frequently putts very poorly and adds more strokes to his score.

On golf telecasts, we have seen professional golfers, superstars like Jack Nicklaus and Lee Trevino, miss putts no longer than two feet. It demonstrates that even the best of golfers do miss short putts.

The really fine golfers, however, do not miss very often. On the green, a good golfer is a picture of concentration, precision, and discipline. He or she looks over the putt from every angle, measures it so as to know exactly how far it must be stroked. He or she judges the break, because those nice smooth greens are not nearly as level as they appear to be from the highway. There are undulations, little curves, and hills. The ball very rarely goes straight, so you have to figure whether it is going to break one direction or another — and how far. You decide whether the putt is uphill, downhill, or sidehill. A good golfer spends much time analyzing and evaluating putts. He or she picks up loose pieces of grass or leaves that are in the path, wanting to be sure that the ball gets close to the hole — or in it.

After all, by par, the basic standard, putting is half the game. The average golf course has a par of seventy two strokes for eighteen holes. Par allows two putts for each of the eighteen greens. Eighteen times two is thirty-six, and thirty-six is half of seventy two. So half the game is on the green; half the game is with the putter.

The following is an account of a man who was golfing with a friend. The friend also played quite frequently with the preacher, and the preacher was with them on this particular day.

On the very first green, this fellow missed a short putt. He was angry and upset. He swore. Then he remembered the preacher was there. He hushed up, apologized, and tried to calm down.

But on the way to the next tee, he slipped up to his friend and whispered, "Doesn't the preacher ever get mad? What does he do when he misses a short putt?"

The friend replied, "When he misses a short putt and gets

mad, he spits — and where he spits, the grass never grows again!"

Now in the game of life, most of you have gotten off the tee (you have started the Christian life). You have gone down the fairway (the straight and narrow). You have listened to the warnings of Jesus (when he shouted, "Fore"). You have emerged through the traps and bunkers (the undesired hazards of life). Most of you are on the green.

But this is no time to relax. This is no time for complacency. Now you need all the concentration and all the discipline that is available. You are still not done; you have got to finish out. You cannot let up. Let us use some Scripture illustrations of how this works in life.

Solomon

Remember ihe story of King Solomon. Solomon was probably the greatest king of Israel, as far as power and prestige, wealth and splendor, are concerned. Under Solomon, the kingdom of Israel reached its largest extent, geographically. Under Solomon, the influence of Israel was world-wide, in the world of that time. Jesus himself said, "Consider the lilies of the field, how they grow; they neither toil, nor spin; yet I tell you, *even Solomon in all his glory* was not arrayed like one of these." (Matthew 6:28, 29)

"Even Solomon in all his glory" — from the lips of Jesus — is a description of the reign of this king.

Take a look at the man. He built a magnificent temple; it took seven years to complete. By our standards today, it cost about six billion dollars.

When that temple was dedicated, the king offered a prayer. That prayer of dedication is a classic, a masterpiece. It is found in 1 Kings, chapter 8. Read the whole thing for yourself.

At the very beginning of his reign, Solomon was a humble and devout person. Soon after his coronation, God appeared to Solomon in a dream and said, "Ask whatever you want; it will be yours."

Solomon's answer revealed his character, "Lord, I don't deserve the position I have. Give me an understanding heart; make me the kind of king that you want me to be" (1 Kings 3). His wish was granted.

That is King Solomon — a true servant of God, a man of devotion and humility, a man of reverence, a man who had it made.

But alas, he changed. He became careless and complacent, neglectful and self-sufficient, lustful and self-indulgent.

He made alliances with many foreign nations, to consolidate the kingdom he had built. His love of luxury and pleasure led to deterioration and compromise. He degenerated into lust and sensuality. He accumulated 700 wives and 300 concubines — marrying pagan princesses to further his political and economic purposes. This led to idolatry and apostasy; heathen temples were erected to many false gods (1 Kings 11:1-8).

Extravagance and waste and corruption were rampant. Enormous taxes had to be levied. (Does all of this sound like the twentieth century?) The taxation burden during the time of Solomon became unbearable; ultimately it led to rebellion and civil war (1 Kings 12).

That's what happened to this fine man who had such a splendid start. He relaxed; he let up; and as a result, he started his kingdom down the path of self-destruction.

Hezekiah

A similar illustration is found in King Hezekiah. He was the king in the southern kingdom when the northern kingdom fell to the Assyrians.

"Don't you ever wonder whether having all those wives was worth it?"

Hezekiah instituted a great reform movement. He brought the people back to God. He cleansed the temple. He initiated a moral and spiritual revival.

Take a quick look at Hezekiah. Soon after conquering the northern kingdom, the Assyrians surrounded the city of Jerusalem. Sennacherib, ruler of Assyria, sent in his ultimatum: "Surrender — or else."

Hezekiah consulted the prophet Isaiah. Hezekiah prayed fervently. And God spared the city of Jerusalem. None of its people died. The army of the great Sennacherib started home the following day — because of a terrifying plague God sent into the camp (2 Kings 18, 19).

At another time in his life, Hezekiah became sick, very sick. Isaiah the prophet came to him and said, "Hezekiah, set your house in order; you're going to die."

"I'm not ready to die," said Hezekiah, "give me some more time."

He prayed — earnestly. He went to the Lord and asked him to spare his life a little longer. And the Lord heard his prayer. Isaiah had hardly reached the court of the temple when God turned him around and sent him right back to the king. Isaiah said to Hezekiah, "God has heard your prayer; he is going to spare your life; he will add fifteen more years." (2 Kings 20:1-11)

That is the kind of a man King Hezekiah was — a man of prayer, a spiritual leader as well as a political monarch.

However, we learn that he relaxed, he let up. He was a man of God; he had it made. But pride, vanity, and self-sufficiency entered his experience.

What happened? A group of Babylonian envoys came to look over his kingdom. And he showed them everything — all the wealth, all the gold and silver, all the ivory and cedar. He showed them all the treasures that the kingdom possessed. He wanted to impress them. He did.

Later on, they came back — with their armies — and took it all home with them.

For his conceit and boastfulness, Hezekiah was rebuked severely by Isaiah the prophet and by the Lord. He had it made. But he trusted alliances with other nations rather than the Lord. He exalted himself and his achievements and his possessions — rather than God.

Judas

Let us turn to the pages of the New Testament for another example. Remember a man named Judas? Judas Iscariot? Who could have had more privilege than that man? For three years he lived in close relationship with the Lord Jesus Christ, the Savior of man, the eternal Son of God. He listened to the parables. He witnessed the miracles. He heard the teachings of Jesus. He enjoyed the fellowship of the disciples. Who had more opportunity than he? How fortunate he was. He had it made.

But he was poisoned by his desire for money. He ended up betraying Jesus — with a kiss.

All of this indicates that there is no end, in this life, to the Christian experience. We need to keep on keeping on.

You're on the green. But that's no time to relax. You're on the green. But you haven't holed it out yet. There is still more to be done.

Two Texts

From the New Testament there are two texts which apply — to the golfer and to the Christian. Each is appropriate — in golf and in life:

1. the words of Paul, "Let anyone who thinks that he stands take heed lest he fall." (1 Corinthians 10:12) A word of warning.

2. the words of Jesus, "He who endures to the end will be saved." (Matthew 10:22) A plea for perseverance.

A Call To Discipline

These two texts — and this message — constitute a call to discipline, a quality that is so uncommon today, yet an attribute so necessary in the Christian experience. How imperative and compelling that we develop habits of discipline as we seek to follow Jesus.

Indeed, the word "discipline" is derived from the same root as the word "disciple." A disciple is a person of discipline.

Yet how frequently we disregard this truth and become easy-going and complacent in our faith. We tend to coast along, completely satisfied with ourselves, seeing no need for developing the discipline which will enable us to grow, to deepen as Christians.

The religious groups which are flourishing and increasing in numbers are those which require discipline from their members. Faithfulness in attendance and regularity in certain practices are basic for these groups. Not only do they expect their adherents to comply with particular patterns — they insist on it.

Seventh Day Adventists practice the discipline of tithing, setting aside one-tenth of their income for their church.

Jehovah's Witnesses practice the discipline of door-to-door visitation, affirming and sharing their faith.

Mormons practice the discipline of dedicating themselves for a two-year period of missionary effort, at their own expense.

These are the religious units which continue to accelerate in membership — and in influence.

Mohammedans practice the discipline of prayer, prostrating themselves before Allah five times daily.

Buddhists practice the discipline of meditation, spending long hours in contemplation and reflection.

We have no right to ridicule any of these until we are willing to do as much for our faith as they do for theirs. We take our faith for granted. We are casual and indifferent. We relax in self-satisfaction and carelessness.

Our lack of discipline will lead us to drifting, to doubt, to failure. How can we look down upon those who give themselves so whole-heartedly to their beliefs? They put us to shame with their zeal and their commitment. Surely we ought to do voluntarily what is mandatory for them.

It was Jesus who said, "Unless your righteousness exceeds (and ours doesn't even equal) that of the scribes and Pharisees, you will never enter the kingdom of heaven."(Matthew 5:20)

Christians today are in need of discipline. We need to work at developing the Christian virtues, the Christian graces, the Christian habits.

We need to "go on to maturity." (Hebrews 6:1) We need to "press on toward the goal for the prize of the upward call of God in Christ Jesus." (Philippians 3:14) We need to strive to reach "the stature of the fulness of Christ." (Ephesians 4:13)

Jesus needed to pray. It is written that he went off by himself, or up into a mountain, or out into the wilderness — to pray. If Jesus felt the need for prayer, who am I to think I can get along without it?

Jesus needed to worship. Regularly, "he went to the synagogue, *as his custom was,* on the sabbath day." (Luke 4:16) If Jesus felt the need for going to church, who am I to think I can get along without it?

Jesus needed to study his Bible, the Old Testament. He knew it well. Over and over, he would quote from it, saying, "It is written . . . " (Matthew 4:4, 7, 10) If Jesus felt the need for knowledge of the Scriptures, who am I to think I can get along without it?

Let us, who name his name, learn to practice the disciplines which Jesus practiced.

Let us, who seek to follow him, learn to develop the holy habits which Jesus developed.

Let us, who would be his disciples, try to make essential in our daily living what Jesus made essential in his.

R. BLAINE DETRICK is a retired United Methodist clergyman. A graduate of Drew Theological Seminary, Madison, New Jersey, he is the father of two grown children. Detrick served pastorates in Parkersburg, Huntington, and Wheeling, West Virginia; Slippery Rock, Pennsylvania; and Lakewood, New York. Beyond his interest in golf, he also pursues an interest in travel. He and his wife Marguerite have hosted twelve tours to locations as diverse as the Holy Land, Hawaii, the Mid-East, and most European countries. The Detricks live in Egg Harbor, New Jersey.